Kingdom of Empty Bellies

by

Kei Miller

Kingdom of Empty Bellies

First edition © The Heaventree Press 2005
All poems © Kei Miller 2005
All rights reserved
ISBN 0-9548811-2-5

The cover image is 'Witness to a Ritual' from the *Revival Series*,
© Bernard Hoyes, 1996

Cover designed by George Ttoouli

Heaventree logo designed by Panna Chauhan

Printed in the UK by
Cromwell Press, Trowbridge, BA14 0XB

Published in the UK by
The Heaventree Press, PO Box 3342, Coventry, CV1 5YB

Thanks to the editors who have published some of these poems. A gre
many of them have appeared in the pages of *The Jamaica Observer's* litera
supplement, *The Literary Arts*. 'Mourning' and 'Noctiphobia' appeared
The Caribbean Writer. 'Hats' and 'Take Off' in *The Paumanok Review*. 'Th
Poem Was Written With Salt' in *Snow Monkey*. 'Onions' (as 'Onion Therap
and 'How the Widow is Remade' in *The Glut*. 'Communion,' 'Uphil
'Marching,' 'Psychopath' and in *The Alsop Review Anthology One*.

Kingdom of Empty Bellies

by

Kei Miller

Published by The Heaventree Press

Contents

Part One: Church Women

Part Two: In Dream Country

Part Three: Rum Bar Stories

for Billson,
for the artists,
for the emptiness
and the kingdoms inside it

*For out of your bellies shall flow
rivers of living water*

—John 7:38

Them belly full, but we hungry

—Bob Marley

Part One: Church Women

when the earth breaks
down to sand

the sand is swallowed
by ocean

the ocean rises
dry to the sun

and the sun has burnt
itself out

she will still be
singing Allelu singing

Allelu singing Allelu

Alleluia

Mother

Because of her mountain breasts
she has learnt a peculiar walk.
a duck-stride to balance herself.
It is hard to see anything
but the stern shifting of those mountains
when in flat, battleship shoes
she marches across the aisle
reaching for sinners, whom she crushes
to her chest, shouting, *Jesus!*
Jesus! until the evil breaks
and the repenter has sprung
a river in the valley of her bosom;
until his spirit-child is born
and nursing.

She has learned the heaven-language
of groans; how
to push and labour for us
even after our birth; how
to sprinkle holy water
on our would-have-been apocalypse.
Each Sunday she reports,
earthquake-style, *Me and the devil*
did have to fight for you soul
again!

In the evenings, she is knitting
the earth – hemming us in,
holding us fast.

Hats

In a Sunday museum of felt
and straw, a boy will be wedged
between fat women, adrenalin bubbled
up into his eyes – he will look
to the stiff circles of mesh, ugly
on the ladies' hats and think
of satellite antennas
catching signals from Heaven.

And child-logic being, 'crowns
are chiselled from blocks of gold,
tattooed with ivy vines,
stippled with blue diamonds,'
the boy will not see the majesty
in these women;
he will not understand
their purple claim:

We not God's children!
We are his wives.

Tongues I

When, during worship, the song ripens
and lyrics become inadequate,
women will strip Britain
off their tongues, allowing them to dance free;
to reach down the spirit-well
and bring back domed ceilings,
crystal windows, Roman columns, marble tiles.

Cabala-builders, the women
erect castles in which God
will reside, while the men watch
and stay outside.

Fasting

In corn and water years, women
learn the art of do-without;
how to stretch cornmeal porridge
for the children, give the man
the last piece of hardough bread;
how to oil away white squall
from their own mouth corners
living instead on every word
that proceedeth from the mouth of God.

On dry Sundays
when their kingdoms of empty bellies
groan, God might be moved
to mercy, and open
his hands for them.

Take Off

She closed her eyes tight
against the unbalancing,
reciting the careful instructions
that might save her life
if the plane stalled in flight.

But the sharp lifting disturbed
her horizontal comfort;
in that tummy-twisting moment
she erupted – pentecostal frenzy,

ballistic shooting psalms,
we were certain she had gone
mad. Perhaps the ascension brought her
too close
to God.

Caught up

Tennessee introduced them
to mountainless land;
to thunderclouds that could sprout
funnel legs and stomp
war for miles.

The women marvelled
at street lights caught up
in a cycle of worship: falling
prostrate, then rising.
But the tornado turned
and huffed at their motel door.

If you can imagine the terror
then you might understand
the praying mother
who ran outside seeking Jehovah
help; you might see the beauty
in her raised arms; in her screaming
and spinning and spinning.

Communion

for whoever eateth and drinketh unworthily,
eateth and drinketh damnation to himself
                                                —I Cor. 11:29

This morning, Geraldine must repent;
a root of bitterness has been spreading
in her heart. Sunday after Sunday, no one
has said Amen to her precise arrangements
of spathodia and daisies. Even the Easter bouquet,
sunflower rising tall from a crowd
of aralia, more poignant than any resurrection
sermon, did not draw the Hallelujahs
she expected.
Kneeling for bread,
she must let the anger fall away like yellow
leaves. Geraldine looks beyond the parson,
to the red flowers laid at the altar
and imagines her sweet Rose of Sharon,
Lily of the Valley, beautiful crown
of Bougainvillea thorns in his head;
how he too sweated blood in the Garden;
and all through history people just have
no appreciation!
     Geraldine swallows, repents.

Uphill

Sister Maisy must walk uphill to church,
dirt road rising sharp as a steeple,
past the rum bar always full
of heathen people, like her husband.
But Maisy walks straight, knows Heaven
is a place that don't reach easy –
but step by step in pink bathroom slippers
that make the uphill softer
on her feet. Maisy dreams on a place
flat as lake water; day and night
she meditates on
the scripture promising
valleys to be exalted and every mountain
to be made low.

Shouting

When the sister scream
like duppy was riding
her, and the big
church brothers had to
hold her down, and
even their muscles used
to farm work couldn't
stop the flouncing that
had the girl's purple
frock flitting and flatting
and making her look
indecent, when all the
women see this carrying-on,
and they start to
shake their tambourines, shake
their rattles, shake their
shack-shacks, when they start
to bob their heads
from side to side
and shiver holy-like,
when they raise up
their hands trembling to
the wood eaves where
Rat and God live
side by side—

it wasn't no joke, it wasn't black people
making monkey of themselves;
it was the Spirit running
hot lava inside of women,
Spirit, like steam
inside a pressure-cooker begging
to come out. Spirit burning
their tongues, making them
have to shout.

War Dance

Whenever Sister Sybil raise the red banner
the air change.

Whenever the flag flash bright
in each woman's eye,
the colour of Jesus' blood

the colour of Satan and sin

the colour of their husbands' fornication,
the air change.

Demons fly out the place
because a woman's screaming is like
a machete blade banging
against the pavement and
evil spirits don't like
the argument of metals.

Whenever sister Sybil raise the red banner
the temperature change, the tempo
change, the mood change

and inside that place, God
begin to happen.

Psychopath

You will not suspect her –
lazy eyes, a soft equator
of waist and the peach floral dress
which like a miracle contains it.
She does not seem the type
to put her mouth on wounds
and suck—

Yet how serenely she speaks
of crushed bodies, plucked beards
and cat-o-nines – how sweetly
she sings of a fountain filled
with blood.

Off-key I

She did not trust the pastor's wife, didn't
believe a woman with squinted eyes could see
Heaven and the Glory, much less reveal
it to her. And she did not like how
the tiny woman, baton raised, would lead
the choir to fold songs, crease them under
then over, form them into peacocks
       or spiders.

She didn't trust these Anansi harmonies
crawling up her shoulders, as if to keep
her down; the church woman would lift her voice
(it could only manage one note)
and power it through the ceiling
until old sisters
added their own
crocus-bag sounds.

The chorus floats like newspaper
up to God's heaven where,
smiling, He adds it to His fold.

Tongues II

Beware of the church woman; her tongue
sharp like serpent.

Under the shade of a broad Sunday hat,
eyes brimstone burning,

she will town-cry the soft secret rising
in Martha's unmarried belly;

gong-mouthed, she will call down
Heaven-healing

for the lewd cancer dancing
inside Billy.

With her, rumours digest easy
into sermons;

Beelzebub salivates on her tongue,
disguising himself as God.

Hallelujahs

The pastor brought lightning.
His odd alchemy combined
Jesus words with newspaper
clippings, sparked
a storm in his mouth –
electrons bounced from filling
to filling, gathered in voltage,
ready to charge out.

The church woman brought thunder
compressed in her belly.
She stood, arms wide,
presenting the barren lands
of her stomach.
She shouted *Hallelujah!*
and called the lightning forward.

Off-key II

The police never knocked or shouted
Open Up! or flashed their warrants;
(things don't work like that here)
just boots and the door collapsing –
a confused woman holding her nightie
at the place where a sagging breast
would fall out; rubbing eyes against
the blackness (she thought it was her soul)
and the words *Jeeee Zus* was rising
out of her belly. Her son was calling
Mamma, and only when the baton hit her
she knew she had stood to save him.

That night the woman learned
how to put Heaven in her voice
how to prophesy – call down Armageddon,
flood-water, twenty plagues on Babylon – how
to bawl down Jericho or sing *It Is Well*
even though the ground refuse to shake
and the jail-walls don't turn to dust and the locks
don't break – even though
her son not coming out.

Each Sunday, the woman finds herself
in church, singing the wrong key –
Egypt and Israel are heavy
on her tongue and push the notes off-centre.
Her song will rise to the Saviour, but might bang
against the padlock of His heart.

Mourning

The church woman is waiting
is waiting, is waiting

through the pin-drop silence.
She lean over to kiss
the starched face, and everyone
hold back their tears
to make space
for her grief.

But the church woman is waiting
is waiting, is waiting

through the pastor's 'him gone
to a better place' sermon.
She don't even nod or lift
her hands in amen
or anything else to pretend
she find comfort
in those words.

The church woman is waiting
is waiting, is waiting

for the service to done
the coffin to be rolled out,
put in the ground.

She is waiting for two shots
of white rum, she is waiting on drums –
and then don't mind the high heels
or the heavy linen
dress, not made for movement,
the church woman will lift her elbows
like scarecrow, knock her knees
and dance and dance and oh lord

him gone!

Testimony

Bredren and sistren, now I know
Almighty God is just a johncrow
Tell me why else would he
Come down for a dead dog like me?

Jubilate

When the preacher let go
of the Sunday women he had held
in his own abracadabra

the music floated
down on john crow wings
and caught them

pressed a feathered finger
to their head-tops and spun them
like pocomania.

The sisters, unwound, hinged
their souls between God and earth –
allowed their hips to swing

wild and unholy. They
rested their heads in Jesus' lap
while their bodies remembered
old time bacchanal.

Marching

It is more than the fear of whale bellies
that keeps her walking.

Give honour to the woman who marches
around Kingston, bearing her banner,

a stout witness: REPENT JESUS SOON COME.
Give honour for the role she played

marching behind Carnival drums,
her own slow time and tune;

for each mile surrendered
as a widow's mite; for her starched dress –

who knew the armour of God was cotton and light?
For the Holy Ghost, Paul Bogle's ghost,

and all the freedom spirits inside her;
for faith which can stand the bruising

weight of sun, which stretches
longer than roads. Each dawn

the woman wields a marker, brightens
the letters on the placard she will raise

like a chorus, like a shout. She is saving
her voice for Jericho.

Death

If the church woman could talk
she would tell you it's not alright,
the place too cold – it have
too much light, too much quiet.

When the church woman closes her eyes
she sees a blue-frocked Sunday choir,
hears groaning, the ecstatic thuds
of their fainting; she feels fire.

If the church woman had strength
she would rip the I.V. out her arms –
nightdress billowing, she would run:

let them sound an alarm.
  Make the saviour find me sprawl out
        on the pavement;
    make them push trolleys to meet me,
        one whole heap of noise.
Make them scream. Sound the sirens.
Let ambulance lights flicker
        like flame, like pentecost,
  like hallelujah

Part Two:
In Dream Country

This traffic this
evening moving slow
making everything slow
except our patience.

Boiling in the sun-hot car,
we thinking about
roads and years —

how it taking so much
and so long
to reach nowhere.

Granna's Eyes

1.

Is de ocean
de blue blue ocean
in mi eye, in mi eye
Is de ocean
de endless ocean
in mi eye, in mi eye

There's a strangeness in her
house – symbols chalked
out on the floor,

never sure what they mean
but you know enough
to not smudge them;

is the smell of hibiscus and olive
oil, the calabashes of water set out
don't care how you complain

bout mosquitoes breeding;
is the way Granna have no one
to pass the evening with

women not easy around her –
always have things to do,
church to go, pastor to see,

reputations to keep
up. When visitors come, the faces hide
behind sunglasses or in the shadow

of hats. They tell her how
they don't deserve this trial or that,
how bad luck seem to find them.

Granna pours sweet oil on their feet,
brush their bodies with tamarind leaves,
she will whisper verses, cancel curses.

And looking up, the visitor might wonder
how come this Mother have blue eyes?

> *Is de ocean*
> *de blue blue ocean*
> *in mi eye, in mi eye*
> *Is de ocean*
> *de endless ocean*
> *in mi eye, in mi eye*

2.

In June, we pick fruits and bright
flowers, pack the basket
till we can barely carry it.

We walk towards the sea
where the cries of hungry pelicans
echo inside our empty bellies.

We march in, salt-soaking our skirts
and Granna take each fruit,
give it to the ocean with a smile.

I spin around with a feeling
like I standing inside her eyes:
the waves, the green, the blue

have, in truth, a strange resemblance.
In June, when Granna answer my question,
I know she answering true –

> *Is de ocean*
> *de blue blue ocean*
> *in mi eye, in mi eye*
> *Is de ocean*
> *de endless ocean*
> *in mi eye, in mi eye*

3.

Some nights are hard to sleep –
the cot keeps rolling and even
when I force it still,

I have that same feeling of being pushed
and pulled, and I wake up breathing hard
and sweating, like is not me one

in the room. Like is plenty, plenty of us
packed in and suffocating, and I hear
the whole village,

their dirges like a huge current
of blackpeoplesinging.

One night when too many
nightmares were crowding in,
I screamed

and Granna came.
But every word turned to dust
in my throat –

Granna's eyes was black
like charcoal.

How come your eyes not blue?
How come it don't
have the ocean inside it?

Is de ocean
de dark night ocean
in mi eye, in mi eye
Is de ocean
de endless ocean
in mi eye, in mi eye

When it is hard to sleep,
when the cot keeps rolling,
look into Granna's eyes

you will see night, no moon,
but stars, and the sea, and a ship sailing
on that same current of blackpeoplesinging;

you will feel sadness bigger than the ocean.
you will see silhouettes on deck
considering how soft

the Atlantic is, and deep will call
to deep and they will jump.
You will see the tears – the hopeless

bawl spreading out across
her face before
she turns it away.

And you will know
that all these years
she been drowning.

Granna, will you keep the ocean
forever?

4.

The day Granna screamed
an ugly, sick-dog sound
like she was vomiting out devils

I did not go inside, because the sound
had chalk drawings and brown
calabashes of water;

it had the smell of hibiscus, old-woman
loneliness and scriptures, bush
medicine, floating mangos,

orange blossoms; it had twenty million
drowned Africans rotting inside it.
I did not go inside

because Granna was breaking
plates and glasses and tables.
Bawling and bawling.

The house was pouring water, heavy
like storm-rain off the roof –
like every pipe had burst,

then, the smell of salt.

> *Is de ocean*
> *de blue, blue ocean*
> *in mi eye, in mi eye*
> *Is de ocean*
> *de endless ocean*
> *in mi eye, in mi eye*

5.

She told me after
how inside she was rising;
that she knew sorrow

must finally end.
And even while ocean ran
from her eyes, through house

and through village –
in the sudden flood, people
all over lost their footing,

splashed into the water
like baptism – even then
she was rising,

her feet planted on two waves
like Jesus. There is a time to drown
and a time to walk on water.

The ocean too has its end.

Aquaphobia

for my mother

An aunt tells me my mother was once afraid
of drowning. She was small and the aluminium basin,
filled for washing lice out of country
children's hair, made her panic, run
naked bawling to Drummily Church. But
it's my mother who taught us to swim –
threw us in the deep
end of pools, worried
that we never cried, never
floundered. *You might drown,*
she said, *if your limbs don't
fight the water.* And all
these years, we have floated on her faith.
She gave her children Jesus-feet
to walk on top of waves.

Noctiphobia

for my grandmother

Because she was wife to the tall preacherman, pentecostongued,
whose every word whipped fire, whose oiled thumb

pressed on women's foreheads made them wheel and turn
then turn again like dogs under the spell of their own tails

and because she wore the gold ring he bought
with Yankee dollars earned from digging through Panama

and they lay on a cot in a cool red house with bamboo
doors, never locked, a devilman stole in

one night, women's jealous money in pocket,
cemetery dirt in hands which he rubbed

onto her belly; each time my grandmother swelled
with child an iron tide rose and drowned the baby.

Six times she felt a sudden stillness at midnight,
learned how to vomit out the fetus

but my grandmother believed curse-breaking magic
lived in the number seven. The familiar

motion of a being inside sent her marching up
to riverhead to sprinkle her belly with water.

My father was christened with seven names
all meaning, 'de lion who bruk up de chains'

and he is a tall preacherman, pentecostongued
whose every word whips fire. The devilman is dead,

choked on fishbone when he saw my grandmother approach,
baby sucking from her tit. But I only remember her

shivering on a cot, singing, *Why should I fear*
de night or de pestilence which walketh inside it?

On Arson and Parachutes

The day after Charlie left
Aunt Valda sat in the blackened shell
of her house, smoke rising
like a benediction to God. Her statement
to police was: I did love him.

At family dinners she was the one who danced
always in a new red dress
and hugging her, the sharp smell
of kerosene would rise as a ghost
from behind her ears.

One Valentine's when I was too young
and too old to say I love you, straight-faced –
I gave her, instead, a balloon.
She laughed then let it go,
watched it settle against the ceiling.

Today, twenty years later, two men
are gliding up over Jack's Hill, soft
against the midday: their parachutes
red and beaming as if the sky
now owns a heart.

I watch them and remember Aunt Valda.
Theirs is the gift I never had to give her:
the ability to rise; the way to fill
lungs with grief, hold it,
and never burst.

Onions

When she died you fell in love with onion rings.
Blessed by the sound of oil popping in her kitchen
again, the calm whisking of eggs, sifting flour
with paprika, triple baptism of each ring.

How you've grown addicted to the slow smoke
which fills the air something like a séance.
Imagine you, who burnt bread religiously
on her birthdays, have found a sudden knack
for gourmet and the delicate use of knives,

have found therapy in the slicing
of white bulbs, the careful release
of fumes –
another excuse,
each day, to cry.

Advice for my Sister Visiting Trinidad

Close your eyes until
the mangoes start smelling like home –
It's easy to forget where you are.
Listen to the women talk
and soon you will hear her –
Mauleen. Open your eyes, adjust
them to Arima market, and no,
it wasn't her at all!
Probably a fat woman, fish crowded
between her legs, arguing with a fellar
about the price of snapper.
But sis, ain't it strange
being in this place
Mauleen's voice has always remembered?

Caribbean Bass

for Shauna

That morning in Boston
when the cold so deep it reach inside
her, it opened up a feeling
like she needed to be home
And what she wanted most
was the bass – for she remember
on the island, when party was keeping
even two or three miles away
how you could feel the riddim,
the bass, it would carry clear-clear
to her patio and everyone knew
a fire was catching, a vibes
was building in that dance –
a reggae vibes, a third world vibes
like you could dance all night.
She would think of her ancestors
how they spoke across plantations
with drums – she wonders
if the DJ at them parties
was telling her something:
Dance girl dance! Life is a bitch!
When she wake up that morning
she had a feeling, like
if she didn't go home
she would die.

"This is an apology…"

to the Trinidadian woman who exclaimed:
Then you does do it in the light?
Yours was a kind of lovemaking that excluded
the sight of each others' tortured faces,
excluded fingernails and the act of crashing
into headboards. Yours was the kind never done
in cane fields or at noon. Yours, the undiscovered
clitoris. I am sorry for the brazenness
with which the young speak of scented candles
and red bulbs – the way we have illuminated
the in and out of sex. Sorry, for the dried skeleton
of desire it must have awoken in you. Dear lady,
we could not guess the ritual rolling up of skirt hems
when you allowed him just a few thrusts –
always, always in the darkness. Astonishing,
that your children were fathered by a silhouette.

How the Widow is Remade

She breaks the cemetery
ground to find
her husband's casket,
dislodges a rib
and wears it around her neck.
The ghost already in hell
will not trouble her.
She never hides
the talisman in the depth
of her church frock,
but wears it proud
so it can ward off weak men.
At first there was flesh
clinging to the bone
so she scraped it off
stewed it with cabbage
and ate. Some say
this is voodoo,
but she was only proving
he was always soft.

"The man after church..."

The man after church
him come up to me sudden
want to know if my locks are real –
I want to answer, *No,*
is 20% cotton.

Some people fraid
of this continent growing in my head
they been walking from Africa
all these years
and I bring it too near.

This Poem Was Written With Salt

sprinkled on the paper.
It is about leaving –
the nasty business of departures.

About broken feet, my mother's feet
and though we pray, light candles,
still no sign of healing.
This poem worries
about sugar in blood.

And this poem is hidden
in the jet black hours of morning;
contemplates ocean,
the great salt womb
contracting till it gives birth to a wet
faceless thing – a prophecy,
your destiny isn't here –

it is about our stubborn wounds
summoning maggots, the truth
that we will be meat. It is about
the 'before-dying' and crossroads
and it is about roads and car radios
without signals and dry throats.

This poem is about leaving –

it even begins to, but can't.
It turns around – is cursed
into a monument of salt.

Psalm 151

Give gun salutes unto God
and He will catch the bullets,
string them in a rosary He is making
for the BadMan who don't fear –
whose end has been marked
by a big 'X'.
God don't share His glory.

Bow your head before the Most High
and pass the time by
counting toes.
If you feel
so bright to lift your head,
just know when Him flash a smile
His 14-karat Don Gorgon
glory will blind you.

Never you rebel against Jehovah –
remember his stoutness
and his plentyland(iness)
and his odd love for vengeance.
Remember Lucifer. Remember
the scriptures are true:
if you draw knife onto God,
then He will draw knife on to you.

Upon Reading Martin's Promised Land Speech

To the preacher man who said,
Only when things are dark
enough, can we see stars
I write this time to say
the Jamaican sky is finally
blacker than its people
and many who had lights
hidden under bushels
have put them in their
rightful place –

now from the mountain
the view is a candle ceremony
a huge darkness punctuated with spots of light.
Is people praying this nation
up to God
and calling the sunrise forward.

Pentecost

To those of you
asking bout my fire
wondering if it gone out
don't worry – I just keep it low.
In this world, too many people soak-up,

like Brother B
standing above us
sea water in his hands that trickle down
to our faces, all we tasting is salt.
And him goi stand there til him dead
til all we spirits dead
til the church dead-dead
and we have a huge funeral
to bury everything. But

Brethren,
I going to be at the graveside
anointing the bodies with kerosene oil
and with my fire, that was never out
(only kept low)
I will start a blaze,

Brethren, we will sing on that day of fire
we will learn how to clap hands again
on that day of fire, we will shout
in unknown tongues;
and the left-over water
from the thawing of our spirits
shall pour out of our eyes –
and we will dance our revival
long into that night.

The Bus Driver is Accused of not Wearing Uniform

Traffic Court, Spanish Town, Jamaica.
11:45 am. Judge Marianne James presiding.
How does the defendant plead?

Your honour, I plead guilty to half
the offence – I had on a blue cotton shirt
buttoned up and tucked in

to brown pants, your honour. What's so wrong
in that? Brown pants like the kind
men wear on Sundays,

the kind we travel in –
dignified looking pants your honour
that Gloria just iron the morning.

Is not the navy blue Government
tell us to wear – I know. But the material
they give us so weak

it always sporting holes. I won't drive
in rags, your honour! Mi mother raise me
better than that.

So I plead guilty to shame
and good manners – splashing cologne
on mi chest each morning and

never boring mi ears or growing
mi hair wild like them criminals today
who jump on buses

to hold knives against wi neck.
I notice I don't see them
in court today, I guess

bad bwoy never out of uniform;
always wear the same dirty merino
and cut up shorts, proving

that him come from nowhere
and answer to nobody. Your honour,
I plead guilty

to a pair of brown pants
and having old time ways that say
a man must leave his house

in clothes that don't tear,
clothes he can wear proud
on his Judgement Day.

In Dream Country

On Monday, lions broke
the padlocks, kept to the ground
as they dragged
their orange bellies
out of Hope Zoo.

They hid in mango trees
above a mixed herd of mahogany
cows and horses who felt
the air's imbalance
and galloped to Blue Mountain
hand in hand.

A mountain prophet with wolves
stuck in his throat, met them
on his way down. He was running
to the ramshackle village,
where old West Indian
writers knelt
behind feeble latches.

On Tuesday, a depressed cow
hid her bastard horse child
in a mahogany tree.
          She was tired of his hard gums
chewing on her teats

and besides, she wanted to migrate
          to a pasture
where she would not wait
          horny each night
          for a lean stallion.

          In the evening, V.S. Naipaul
          rode past on a black lion
screaming his condescension, *Fire bu'n*
          for Bob Marley, fire bu'n
          for RastafarI,
firebu'n for King Selassie I

On Thursday, lions burnt
fridges and tires in Miguel Street
        because Wednesday never came.

        On TV-J, a stammering
horse complained,
        How c-c-can we create
without b-b-blood – without b-b-blood –
without bloodclawt consistency?

and the cows cut their dreadlocks
in the Rivers of Babylon –
        dipped themselves under October
swollen waters, and emerged
singing Shango songs.

Friday, an abandoned child forgave
his horse father
      and his cow mother;
lit a candle for Derek Walcott
      and his mulatto poems.

Lions and duppies with wolves
      stuck in their throats
danced a careless bachannal
on thin roads

the latest calypso inside their feet:
      ain't no money, ain't no cents
            left in Dream Country.

Dread

Dreadlocks-rastaman is full of omens;
he's tired of radio's dark prophecies:
the sea still swallows black men.

This morning he listened to the ravens
gathered on power lines making queries.
Dreadlocks-rastaman felt that was an omen.

The news today tells of five fishermen
who sailed out to fill their empty bellies
not knowing the sea still swallows black men.

Bongoman would run and cry to the mountains
but they are off balance – might fall and crush his
dreadlocks. Rastaman is full of omens.

He would write a dub to the government
wailing for four hundred years of tragedies
because the sea has swallowed black men;

he would chant nyabinghi if it made sense
but there are no simple remedies.
Dreadlocks-rastaman is full of omens
and the sea still swallows black men.

(In) a Line Behind Baugh

Eddy, as if the whole morning had to pass
before I reach the counter and the woman
who on Sundays will read my poem and smile
look through me like she don't know me,
look on the papers I fill out – stark
and unbeautiful like a first draft. She explain,
Poetry is not a secure profession. We must deny
your visa application.
                                I keep my mouth shut
for fear I would stammer something unbeautiful
like an unrehearsed reading.
And Lord! This whole wasted day of inching
towards rejection, I could have been
in a lover's arms or writing, and Lord!
it hard, the way a line can break
                                              you.

This Johncrow

This johncrow
flying over Spanish Town bypass
confused, for his bredren
who did sight a dead dog
dipped down to feast in spite
of an oncoming truck.

This johncrow
flying high over Spanish Town bypass
hungry and this pulp of black feathers
this flattened bird with a flattened expression
suddenly look appealing.

This johncrow
wondering if such cannibalism
breaks the rules – but he reason to himself:
It's a dog eat crow,
crow eat dog,
crow eat crow who dip to eat dog world.

A Who Seh Sammy Dead?

in three parts, for the escaped monkey

In July 2002, a monkey escaped from the Hope Zoo
in Jamaica and was found dead, two days later,
under a mango tree. Dogs had killed him.

1. Sammy plant piece-a corn down a gully

...tell them the corn wasn't really corn
but something you seeded, like maybe a dreadlock
from your rebel days in Honduras
hidden in soil so one day you'd remember
the fire
            the anger
                        that some cities are worth burning –
      this was before
they reeled you in with fish net and had you
thrashing a let-mi-guh jungle dance,
khakiman clapping
            dancemonkeydance!
while you were bawling
            muuuuuurrrrrrrtheerrrrrr!
                  or maybe the corn was your navel string –
call it what you will – it was planted
in a gully that wasn't a gully
      but is suh babylon call our homes
cause is not theirs

            Sammy, cómo se dice 'home'
                        en español?

67

2. And it bear till it kill poor Sammy

…tell them the tree, once planted, will bear.
They thought you forgot Honduras,
thought you'd grown accustomed to the monotonous
grid of iron, to St. Thomas bananas and the flat
non-music of our dialect –
    they thought you were content making monkey
faces as trade for Snickers and lollipops,
    content passing collection hats
for blind organ grinders, content to scratch
your balls on camera.

…tell them Sammy, how you finally heard the tree
humming at night – how you've been jungle dreaming
and memories that died in your prison have risen
like Lazarus, zombie arms to choke you.
These past nights you woke crying
for mama
            crying for mambo and merengue and garifuna
                crying *en español*,

    Libertad! Libertad para mi!

3. Sammy dead Sammy dead Sammy dead-o!

...tell them your death is not really death
cause wasn't no shame in it – shame is
breath expired behind bars
      while your brothers find eternity
           in the jaws of cougars.

Your death is not death,
          only the separation of fur from spirit
      the ability to fly
          a monkey dream *en español*
homecoming, party, fiesta.

Your death is amen and amen,
          the swell-up of chains to bursting,
dugu, kumina, *bienvenidos*
          a Honduras otra vez!

A who seh Sammy dead? A who seh Sammy dead?
Tell them...
          tell them...
              Mi nuh dead-o!

"Man who born to drown..."

Man who born to drown can't hang
and man who born to hang can't drown.
                              —Jamaican proverb

– is given the freedom to walk through ghettos after dark, to
  jump out of planes and to climb mountains without rope
– is given the sweet impossibility of dying on highways, trapped
  and bleeding in a crush of metal;
– or of swallowing insecticide stored in soda bottles.

– is also given these warnings: do not spend time on rocks that
  overlook the ocean; deep still calls unto deep. Avoid puddles
  of water and never bathe in tubs. Above all else, drink and stir
  your coffee with a straw. Remember, it is possible to drown

                                        in just a teaspoon.

Psalm 152

To the God who sits
by the Great Wheel thumbing
patterns into wet pots,
our clay bellies have worn thin.
Please restore us.

Part Three:
Rum Bar Stories

#1

Sunset Glow
1 shot coconut rum
2 shots orange juice
Dash of lime juice
1 egg yolk
Blend with crushed ice

In this cool amber night, this warm-Heineken quiet
that have men holding their crotch like they want to piss,
the radio alone is listening
to Ernie Ranglin and his Old Time
Reggae – boogying there on the bass line
as if it was still 1973
and the men slumping
silent on bar-stools had no pot-bellies
or prune-wrinkled wives,
no Friday-Night-Girls
young as their daughters,
no day's end anger
to keep them so quiet.

#2

Liza's Love
1 large shot gold rum
1 large shot triple sec
4 shots pineapple juice
Dash of lime juice
Shake and pour over ice
Garnish with cherry and orange

When the rum stretched itself
into an Atlantic and he
overboard and drowning
came up for breaths,
he never once shouted for help,
but told us instead
of his naked wife spread-eagled
and whimpering under the buck
of a huge black man; he told us
of his surprise blooming
in the doorway, how she opened
her eyes and screamed; he told us
how the man got up slowly,
erect, his testicles swinging,
and walked past him
like it was nothing.

#3

Reggae Sunsplash
1 shot each gold rum and overproof rum
Half shot wild orange liqueur
4 shots pineapple juice
3 shots orange juice
Half shot honey
Blend with crushed ice

She always wondered if the Tuesday jazz
singer who dug clean purple notes
out of cancers, really knew a place
where ain't nobody crying
and ain't nobody worried
and ain't no men
coming in crusted
with a day's leftover of cement,
calling her whichever name
they chose that day, men who ordered
salt peanuts and whites,
sitting for the next five hours drinking
her with their eyes.

She always hummed to the Tuesday jazz,
moving behind the counter like coconut rum
was in her waist, smoothing salt waves
out from her dress. She wanted
to be taken to this place
where ain't nobody crying
and ain't nobody worried
and God willing, ain't no men
there at all.

#4

Gin Gin Mule
Half shot lime juice
Half shot syrup
6 mint sprigs
1 shot ginger beer
1 large shot gin
1 splash soda water
Muddle, shake and pour over ice
Garnish with lime

In this yellow pub, Heineken
banners sigh

off the walls, triangle ears point downward
as if to hell

with this place and these men.
He sits, thumb-stirring dry

gin he'll hardly drink. At times, odd
sensations, a heart-tightening, overwhelm

him; his house is a beige crowd
of disappointments –

drawers of letters bear loud
witness to a world bent

on empty thank yous and iron
rejections. And he, too nervous,

too proud to cry in his wife's
lap, in her ample hug

finds himself in amber dimness
between rumheads who sleep in the cups

they drink from. He understands life
is like this – always cornered, always dogged.

He thumbs a soprano on the glass's rim
knowing it cannot heal him.

#5

Jamaica Dream
1 large shot light rum
1 shot pineapple juice
1 shot orange juice
Shake well
Sprinkle cinnamon on top
Pour over ice

Because Jamaica has too many mountains,
too many hard heights that grow
over men's dreams like grave stones,
when the fellow drinks he lets
the Appleton rise like Flood
to flatten hilltops; to drown
the island rhythm off his tongue;
he ends up with a loose twang

and because this voice is born
from a rebellion at mountain and land,
it sprouts yellow wings and soars above
the unwilling reward of coins trickling
from slot machines, above Ernie
Ranglin's amber reggae, above
every man's story. It soars
like Noah's pea-dove
in search of a coconut branch,
clueless if its wings grow tired
of danger lurking.

#6

Virgin Mary
6 shots tomato juice
Dash of Worcestershire sauce
Dash of Tabasco
Dash of lime juice
Pinch of salt and pepper
Celery
Mix all over ice
Garnish with a lime wedge

Always, when this fellow drink
him see the Virgin Mary peeping
out from the belly of a guitar
and if you tell him, no, you don't see
her, he will pick the instrument
up, let his fingers dance out
a tune that make you see visions
more than Mary or Jesus or angels.

And always, is the same lyrics –
a daughter who died too young,
the balm hours spent on
the veranda of a school teacher

who told him unknown portions
of the child's life.
Lately, he prefers
the school teacher's bed
to his wife's.

And when he is not drunk
ask him to play that same song
and he'll laugh – *Me?*
You telling lies! Boy,
I've never touched a guitar
in my life.

7

Wench
Equal parts amaretto and spiced rum
Shake over ice
Strain into a chilled glass

—to the politricks
that had me busting asphalt
and laying pipes this Good Friday
morning—

                        cheers

—to the red whore
from Clarendon who ate cashews
        in the bahma grass
beside the highway
and who do it with me right
there; that red bitch
who give me syphilis—

                        cheers

—to Sandra who I don't see
in years; who land in New York
on hard times and pawned
our wedding band for bread—

                        cheers

—to this bartender boy
who won't pour me another drink,
won't sell me a next beer – I hope
your balls drop off one day—

                        cheers

#8

Drink & Die
1 shot sambuca
1 shot tequila
4 dashes of Tabasco sauce
Layer in order in a glass

Paul, I coming
but I coming late.
Irene won't leave
me alone until
I read the front page
of the Gleaner and drink
the damn banana porridge.
Then only after she kiss
my forehead, and ask –
*Papa you will behave
youself today?* and I say
yes, does she go
on her business.

So Paul, I coming
but I coming slow.
These days the rum bar
seem further away
than time before when
we was young men returning
from a black day at the tire factory.
And recently, I been losing
my way and is long
after morning done
I finally find myself through
the doors.

Paul, I coming,
please wait on me
and I will tell you
about West Indies cricket,
how Carlooper is our
salvation, and as always
you won't agree with me.
And today, if someone ask
who the hell I talking with –
if I don't know is six years
you been dead now, Paul,
I will hit the brute down –
for not knowing how spirit
and spirit is always talking.

And Paul, these days I feel
my bones being pulled
into the earth
and my skin lifting
to show the duppy-self
underneath. So I know
I coming, Paul, real soon.